3. Chesil beach
4. Spurn Head
5. Blackpool (U
6. Dungeness (
7. Jutland coas
8. Playa de Ca

(Ukraine)

CW01604178

J551.36
Knapp, B
Beach

JB

Items should be returned to the library from which they were borrowed on or before the date stamped above unless a renewal has been granted.

Gloucestershire County Library, Arts & Museums

990815790 6

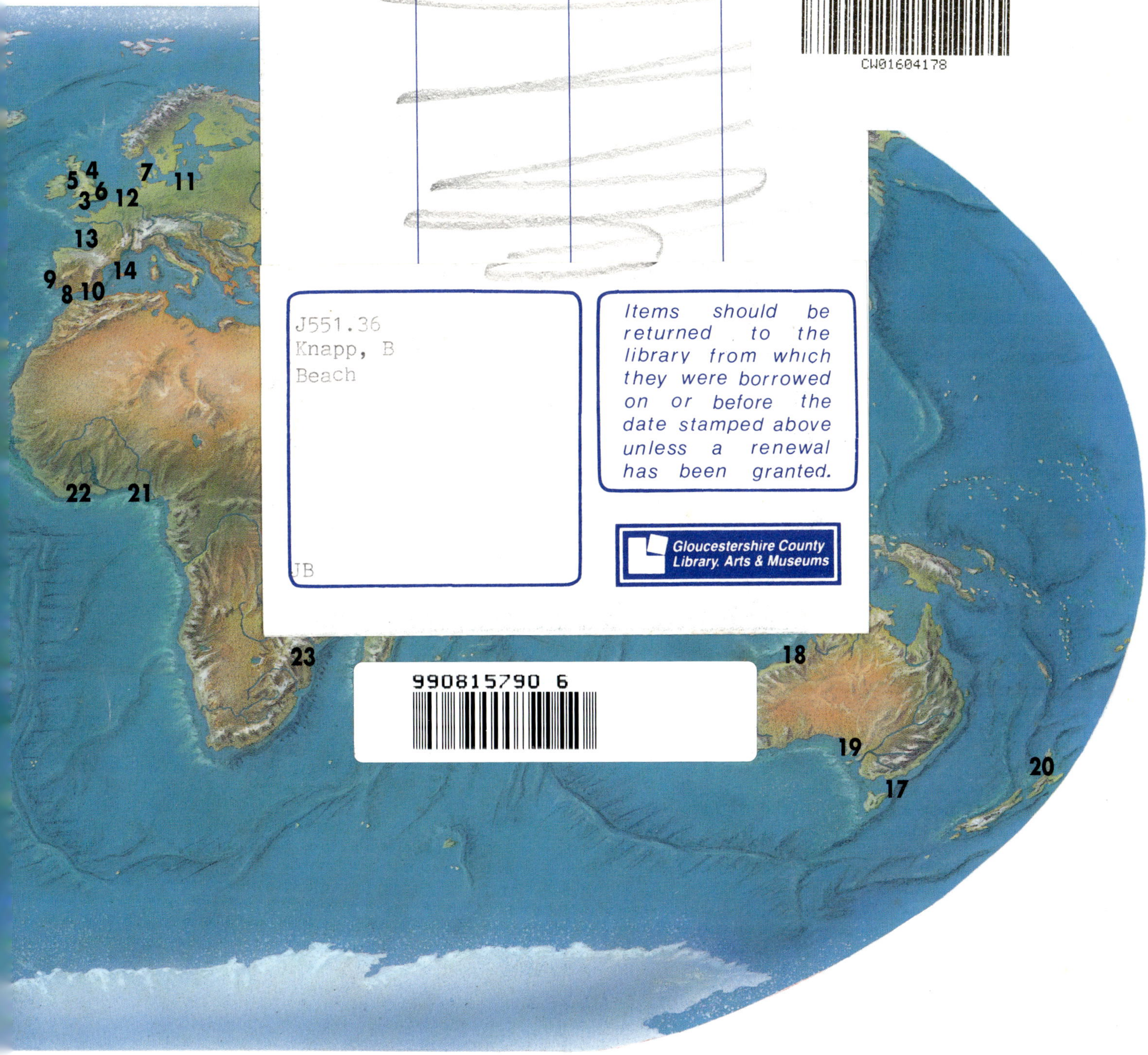

Beaches in Antarctica:
none

Beaches in Australasia:
17. Ninety mile beach (Australia)
18. Eighty mile beach (Australia)
19. Younghusband Peninsula (Australia)
20. Kaipara Harbour/Ninety mile beach (New Zealand)

FACTS ABOUT BEACHES

More than three-quarters of all the people on Earth live on low-lying land near to a beach. Twelve of the biggest 13 cities in the US, for example, are ports; so are all but one of the biggest five cities in the UK and all of the biggest cities in Australia. Indeed, if you choose any country with a coastline and look in an atlas you will find the same pattern.

Some beaches are very wide and stretch seaward for over two kilometres at low tide. The seaside town of Southend in the UK has the world's longest pier. At low tide the supports of all its 2 kilometres are exposed and make up part of the beach.

The world's longest single beach may be Ninety Mile beach in Australia. The longest stretch of beached coast in the world lies off the eastern and southern coasts of the US and Mexico, where beaches on land and in offshore barrier islands like Miami beach stretch for over 3000 kilometres.

One of the world's steepest beaches, Chesil beach, stands at an angle of over 20 degrees and much of its 22 kilometres are made of pebbles. The highest part of the beach is over 20 m above low tide level.

ATLANTIC EUROPE
PUBLISHING

LAND SHAPES

BEACH

GLOUCESTERSHIRE
CLASS
COPY
COUNTY LIBRARY

Author
Brian Knapp, BSc, PhD
Art Director
Duncan McCrae, BSc
Editor
Rita Owen
Special models
Tim Fulford, MA, Head of Design and Technology, Leighton Park School
Illustrator
David Hardy
Print consultants
Landmark Production Consultants Ltd
Printed and bound in Hong Kong
Designed and produced by
EARTHSCAPE EDITIONS

First published in the United Kingdom in 1992 by Atlantic Europe Publishing Company Ltd, 86 Peppard Road, Sonning Common, Reading, Berkshire, RG4 9RP, UK

Copyright © 1992
Atlantic Europe Publishing Company Ltd

British Library Cataloguing in Publication Data

Knapp, Brian
Beach. – (Landshapes)
1. Beaches – Juvenile literature
I. Title II. Series
551.457

ISBN 1–869860–16–0

All rights reserved. No part of this publication may be reproduced, stored in a retrieval system, or transmitted in any form or by any means otherwise, without prior permission in writing of the publisher, nor be otherwise circulated in any form of binding or cover other than that in which it is published and without a similar condition including this condition being imposed on the subsequent purchaser.

Acknowledgements. The publishers would like to thank the following: Leighton Park School, Martin Morris and Redlands County Primary School.

Picture credits. All photographs from the Earthscape Editions photographic library except the following (t=top, b=bottom, l=left, r=right): NASA 14/15, 34/35; ZEFA 8/9, 27.

Cover picture: The Gower, Wales.

In this book you will find some words that have been shown in **bold** type. There is a full explanation of each of these words on page 36.

On many pages you will find experiments that you might like to try for yourself. They have been put in a blue box like this.

In this book km means kilometres and m means metres.

These people appear on a number of pages to help you to know the size of some landshapes.

CONTENTS

World map 2

Facts about beaches 4

Introduction 9

Chapter 1: Where beaches come from

Beaches and bays 10

What beaches are made from 12

The rivers that make beaches 14

Cliffs under attack 16

Where beaches form 18

Chapter 2: How waves shape beaches

In the surf 20

When waves plunge 22

Why sand moves 24

Mud, glorious mud 26

Coastal dunes 28

What tides do 30

Drifting sand 32

Bars and barriers 34

New words 36

Index 37

Take care by the coast

Coastlines are some of the world's most exciting landshapes and you are sure to want to visit them. But never walk close to the edge of a cliff top or swim in the sea without an adult present. Cliff tops often have unstable edges and there may be strong currents just off the beach that can carry you out to sea. Coastlines can be dangerous places for the unwary and deaths have occurred because people have not taken care.

Introduction

A beach is a narrow strip of loose material which is covered and uncovered by the tide. Normally beaches are made of broken rock called **sand**, but some beaches are made of fine mud and others of large pebbles. In the tropics many beaches are also made of broken coral.

Beaches come in all shapes and sizes. Some beaches are no more than pockets of sand, hidden in tiny bays and protected by cliffed headlands of tough rock. Other beaches stand fully exposed to the sea, stretching as far as the eye can see in long sweeping curves.

With every breaking wave, with every change of tide and with every passing storm, beaches change their shape as the beach materials are thrown this way and that by the **energy** of the waves and currents. Yet over the years beaches neither grow nor shrink. They can also stand up to fierce storms which damage man-made things such as homes and roads. They do this by soaking up the energy of the waves rather than trying to resist it.

The world's biggest beaches are immensely long. In Australia, for example, '90 mile beach' is over 140 kilometres in length, while in the United States there are island beaches that fringe the coast for three thousand kilometres.

In this book you can find out about how the world's beaches are formed and how each one has its own story to tell. Enjoy the world of beaches by turning to a page of your choice.

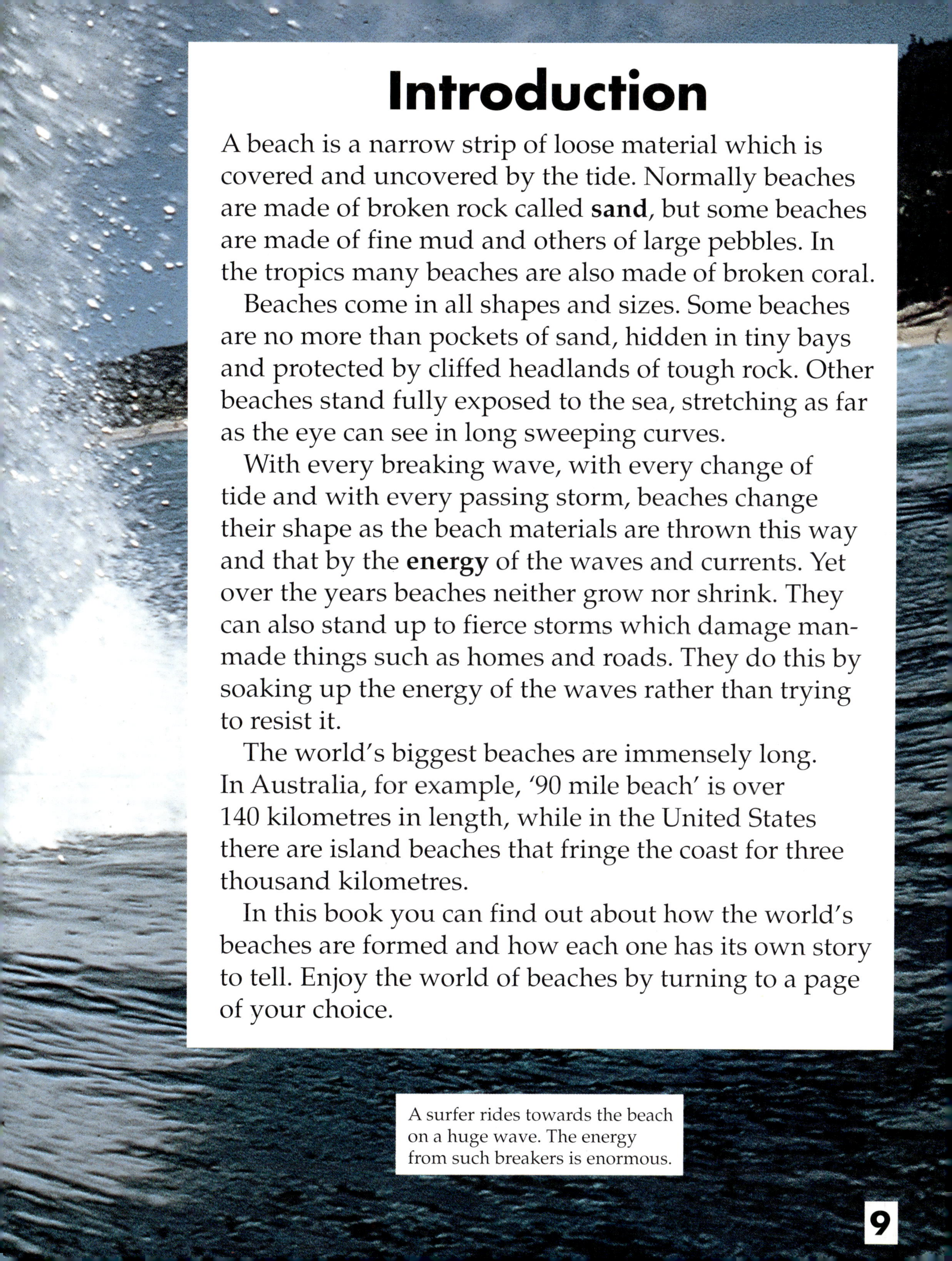

A surfer rides towards the beach on a huge wave. The energy from such breakers is enormous.

Chapter 1
Where beaches come from

Beaches and bays

Beaches are found in many places, some fill in small bays as you can see in this picture. Other beaches can make long narrow bands that separate cliffs from the open sea.

Beaches are constantly on the move but it is not always very obvious. What actually happens may therefore surprise you!

Some sand is carried from the beach by winds to make **dunes**. In this picture the dunes have grass growing on them, but the trails made by people show that sand lies just below the surface (see page 28).

Most of the sand for a beach is brought in by rivers as they **erode** the land (see page 12).

Keeping a balance

There are two sources for the sand on a beach. The most important (although the least easy to see) is sand brought by rivers from the land. More material is added as sea cliffs erode.

The waves, which always seem to be driving onshore, actually carry sand along the shore and then out to sea. And more sand is lost from the beach at low tide when winds whip it up to make sand dunes.

As waves break against cliffs more sand is produced (see page 14).

As the tide changes, the waves rework different parts of the beach (see page 30).

Sand builds up to fill the bay (see page 16).

Sand is building to make a ridge, called a **sand spit**, which is changing the course of the river (see page 34).

What beaches are made from

Beaches are one of nature's dumping grounds.

Sand, is the most common size of material, but there may be other sizes of rock fragment as well. The very smallest particles produce muddy beaches, whereas the larger sizes create pebbly ones. In many places the waves sort the sizes out to give pebbles at the back of the beach, sand in the middle and mud closest to the sea.

A tropical beach with sand of rock grains and coral, Phuket, Thailand.

Where to find different materials

Beaches are made by the waves sweeping back and forth. A beach usually has several parts. Nearest the sea it is flat, and often muddy; nearer the shore it is sandy, while pebbles – if they exist at all – will be found near the back of the beach.

Every beach has its share of shell fragments. With every breaking wave, shells get caught up in the surf zone and are thrown about the beach. This quickly breaks the shells into tiny pieces.

Because shells are so easily broken up by the waves, the animals that lived inside the whole shells you see on a beach must only have died a few weeks before.

Many tropical and sub-tropical beaches are made from sand that has no rock in it at all. Instead it is entirely made from sand-sized pieces of **coral** or shell.

Many of the world's beaches are made of 'golden sand'. Sand has to be tough to stand up to the constant battering as it is thrown back and forth along a beach. A clear glassy material called quartz stands up among the best. The golden colour comes from the rusty stain that occurs naturally in the quartz.

Chesil beach, UK.

Steeply-sloping beaches are usually made from pebbles. These pebbles are of a tough mineral called flint. When the waves move this coarse material up and down a beach it makes a very loud crashing sound.

The rivers that make beaches

The biggest supplies of beach sand come from rivers. Many rivers are coloured brown from the sand and mud they carry, and some send out great plumes of material far into the sea.

The biggest rivers send so much material to the sea that waves cannot carry it away fast enough and a **delta** is formed.

Lowering the land

Rivers are like the veins of the land carrying water to the sea, just as veins in our bodies carry blood back to the heart. Sand and mud that has been eroded from the land is carried back to the sea by rivers to be made into new rocks.

The amount of sand and mud leaving the land is enormous, although it is rarely easy to see.

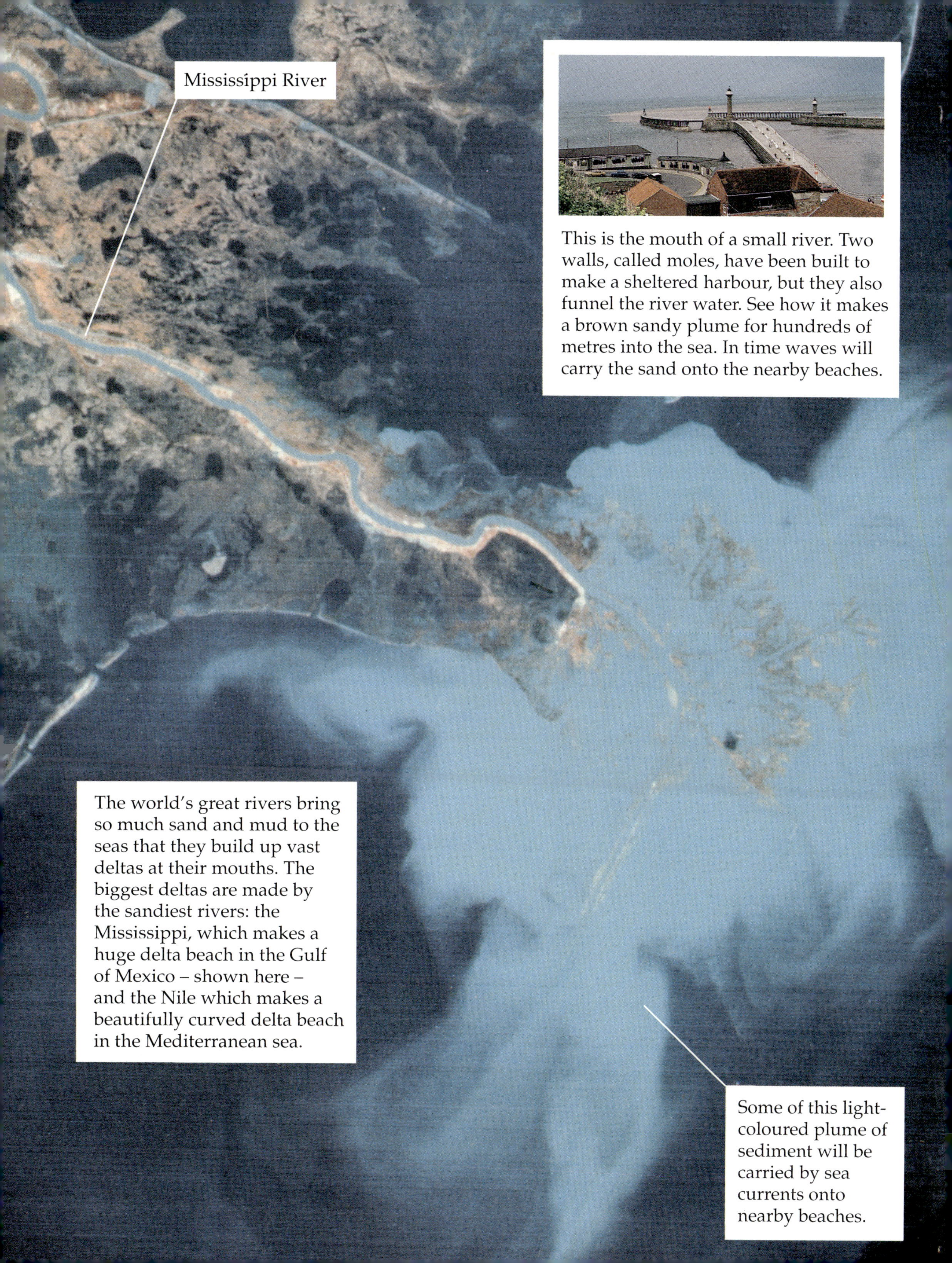

This is the mouth of a small river. Two walls, called moles, have been built to make a sheltered harbour, but they also funnel the river water. See how it makes a brown sandy plume for hundreds of metres into the sea. In time waves will carry the sand onto the nearby beaches.

The world's great rivers bring so much sand and mud to the seas that they build up vast deltas at their mouths. The biggest deltas are made by the sandiest rivers: the Mississippi, which makes a huge delta beach in the Gulf of Mexico – shown here – and the Nile which makes a beautifully curved delta beach in the Mediterranean sea.

Some of this light-coloured plume of sediment will be carried by sea currents onto nearby beaches.

Cliffs under attack

Beaches do not get all of their sand from rivers. Some of it is also produced as waves beat against exposed cliffs.

Beach colours can vary enormously. Often you can trace the colour of the beach material to the colour of the rocks in the cliffs. If the beach sand comes from rocks like sandstone, the sand is yellow. In areas where the cliffs are made from coral the sand is white, whereas if it is made from volcanic **lava** the sand is black.

The cliffs in the picture below are made of hard rock which can withstand the mightiest storm. However, the ragged shape reminds us that the waves are gradually eroding it in places where the rocks are weakest and, in the process, making sand for beaches.

This rocky headland is very exposed and these waves are also too powerful to let the sand settle out at the cliff foot. Waves carry the sand to nearby sheltered bays.

Each time a wave breaks against a cliff, water is forced into cracks in the rock at wave height. This weakens the rock and eventually blocks fall away, often causing the whole cliff face to collapse as well.

Gradually these blocks are broken down further by the pounding waves until at last they are no more than grains of sand.

Where beaches form

Beaches are thin sheets of sand, mud and pebbles that rest on rocky coastal ledges. In some places the rocky ledges are too exposed for the sand to settle and so they remain bare. Elsewhere the waves are not powerful enough to carry the sand away and it smooths over the rocky ledge, making a beach.

Beaches are not very thick and sometimes you can even dig down at spade's depth and find rock. All beaches sit on a ledge, or platform, of rock that has been cut out of the cliffs. In this picture you can see a bay at low tide. The rocks that have been cut away make lines across the shore.

In this place the waves are too fierce to allow the sand to build up and only a thin beach covers the upper part of the platform. However, rocky ledges exist under nearly all sandy beaches.

This beach-level view of the bay shows the headlands in the distance and the wide, flat beach.

The ribs of an old wooden sailing ship show in the front of the picture. It is only partly buried because the beach is not very thick.

The wreck sits on the rock platform below.

In this picture taken from a cliff top you can see the whole length of a bay. Many beaches are found inside bays because the shelter of the headlands makes a good place for sand to settle out.

You can tell that the beach is very wide and much sand must have settled out in the bay by looking at the movement of the waves. Waves only break where the water is shallow, so the width of the breaker zone is a good indication of how wide the beach is.

Chapter 2
How waves shape beaches

In the surf

Some beaches are made by waves. Breaking waves form a churning, tumbling, foaming mass of water called surf and it is within the surf that sand moves up a beach or is dragged back down it.

The forward rush of water from a breaker, called the **swash**, and the return flow of water after the breaker is spent, called the **backwash**, rarely balance out. If the swash is the more powerful then sand is pushed up the beach, but if the backwash is the more powerful then sand moves offshore. These pages show waves where swash dominates.

Spilling waves

If you look at the way the waves in the pictures on this page break you will see that the crests spill forward. These waves are therefore called spilling waves. They are the 'bulldozers' of the beach, pushing sand from the sea on to the beach.

1. A group of people stand watching as a breaker spills.

2. Each breaker spills down on the back of the previous wave, rushing forward as white foaming water called swash.

3. The bravest have stood their ground as the wave moves up the beach. They feel the force of the swash and it almost knocks them over.

4. After the force of the wave is spent the last of the backwash speeds down the beach, dragging sand from beneath toes and setting up a wake. Meanwhile the next breaker approaches.

Beaches and weather

The shape of a wave changes with the weather. Stormy weather produces waves that make a powerful backwash. By contrast fine weather produces waves that have a powerful swash. So a storm followed by fine weather will result in waves first dragging sand from the beach then pushing it back onshore.

Caution:

On a steep beach the backwash, or undertow, can be very powerful and could drag you out to sea. Never stand in the surf zone except on a beach where the 'all-clear' flags are flying and where a life guard is present.

When waves plunge

Plunging waves are mainly found during or just after stormy weather. This is when the waves have their greatest energy, so a short period with plunging waves can very quickly change the beach shape.

Plunging waves curl over and 'rake' sand from the beach, making it flatter and carrying sand out to sea.

Snapshots of waves

One of the best ways of finding out what waves are doing is to take several photographs of them in quick succession. This has been done in the pictures below.

Take pictures on several days and make a record of the weather on each occasion. Then compare the picture sequences to find out if there was any obvious relationship between waves and weather.

This choppy water is typical of a stormy sea. It makes short, tall waves that can plunge on the beach.

A plunging wave seems to rear up out of the sea. There is little sign of its approach. Compare this with the waves shown on page 20.

This is the remains of the previous wave. It is now flowing back down the beach and is called backwash.

Vanishing beach

The greatest amount of beach destruction occurs when a storm hits the beach as the tide is falling. The effect is rather like a rake in a garden. As each wave plunges it drags the sand down the beach, so as the tide goes out the material is pulled a little farther offshore by each new wave.

In a single day a beach can lose over a metre of sand. It has been attacked by the beach destroyers, or plunging waves. After a severe storm beaches may even disappear, revealing their rocky base. However, spilling waves in finer weather will eventually push the sand back onshore again.

Testing the waves

The best way to find out about spilling waves is to stand in the breaker zone and feel the way the water swirls round your feet. When you next visit a beach you might also like to find out about waves this way. However, it is *not* safe to stand in the surf zone of plunging waves like those shown on this page. So first check to see the shape of the wave as well as making sure the 'all clear' flags are flying and that there is an adult on hand.

Strong backwash looks like this.

This is what the crest of a plunging wave looks like.

This is the surf made by the plunging wave. It rushes forward up the beach as swash.

Why sand moves

Sand appears strong and makes sandcastles and firm beaches when it is damp. But sand moves easily whenever waves are on the beach. This is why.

A tray with very little water shows how sand is firm when damp.

Why sand holds water

Sand is made of small grains that do not fit together well. The gaps left between the grains trap water, and the water helps to hold the sand firmly together. This effect is called **surface tension** and it is the force that allows you to make sandcastles.

Surface tension only works when the sand is damp. When sand is completely wet, the surface tension force disappears and the grains can be moved about much more easily.

The same tray with more water in destroys the strength of the sand and it collapses into a flat layer.

Quicksand

If you stand in the surf you may find yourself sinking into the sand. This is a kind of quicksand effect.

To show how quicksand works get a tall glass and place a long tube in the bottom, with the other end attached to a funnel. Fill the glass with sand and then rest a coin on the top.

Add water to the glass from above until it is just level with the top of the sand. The coin does not move because the sand grains are still pressed firmly together.

Now pour some water into the funnel. The coin will quickly begin to sink because the water is flowing upwards from the tube, pushing the sand grains apart and letting the coin move down.

In the breaker zone part of the swash sinks into the beach and flows back to sea through the sand. Where it comes out again under the waves the sand is buoyed up – the quicksand effect. This makes it even easier for the breaking waves to disturb the sand and move it along the beach.

Ripples on a beach.

Ripples show how sand changes

If you walk over the lower beach when the tide is fully out you will sometimes find ripples.

Because the sand is damp, the ripples appear firm to the touch. The ripples were made when the sand was under water as the waves moved back and forth. If you wade across a rippled beach as the waves are breaking you will find the sand in the ripples is easily moved.

Mud, glorious mud

Rivers bring both sand and mud to the coast. However, where waves are strong the mud does not readily settle out along the shore. Instead, the mud settles out where the coast is sheltered, and in these places deep layers of sticky mud are common.

Mud, brought by rivers, settles out as soon as it reaches the quieter waters of an **estuary**. So much is laid down that it has to be dredged from harbours every day.

Unlike sand, mud clings together when it is wet as well as when it is dry. It will even cling to the unwary walkers who venture on to a mud bank at low tide.

Mangroves: trapping the tropical mud

In many tropical and sub-tropical places the coasts are lined with forests of mangrove trees. These trees have tall root systems that trap the mud (see below). So unlike beaches elsewhere in the world, the mud here is found at the top of the beach and the sand is found beyond the mangrove trees.

Where muddy beaches form
Mud does not stick together in the fresh waters of rivers. But as soon as the mud reaches the salty waters of the sea, the properties in the salt begin to make the mud sticky, forming it into a thick mass that will not readily be moved away.

Once the mud builds up above low tide level plants begin to colonise the area and muddy beach becomes land.

Coastal dunes

Coastal sand dunes are formed when wind blows dry sand from a beach onto the shore. Often it is then held in check by the grasses that colonise the sand dunes.

Dunes are like a huge sand reservoir and sea wall combined. They take the full force of giant waves during storms and they are rebuilt during calmer weather.

Without this 'savings bank' of sand, storms would sometimes strip beaches bare and high seas would flood over coastal land.

For more information on sand dunes, see the book 'Dune' in the Landshapes series.

Wind blows onshore from the drying beach at low tide.

Many grasses are able to live in a salty, sandy desert of beach dunes. But they cannot tolerate being trampled on, and if too many people walk across the dunes the grass is soon killed and the dunes will begin to blow away. This is the reason it is important to keep off the areas where the grass is growing.

Sand dunes are found at the back of many beaches and they are vitally important to beach survival.

Sand on the facing side of a dune is loose.

Sand on the landward part of the dune is fixed by growing plants.

What tides do

Beaches owe much of their shape and size to the tides. In countries where the difference between high tide and low tide is small, the beaches are often narrow and poorly formed.

The widest beaches occur in areas where the tidal differences are large. Sometimes such beaches can be more than two kilometres wide at low tide and in these places you will find that the beach has many different zones.

Tidal range

The greatest range between tides occurs twice a month and is called a Spring Tide. This is the best time to see a beach. Half way between each Spring Tide there is a Neap Tide when the difference between high and low tides is quite small.

This is as high as the tide and storm waves ever reach.

This steep slope was made by plunging waves. As the tide was going out sand and pebbles were dragged down the beach. It was made at a Spring Tide.

Steps of tide

If you stand on a beach at low tide and look carefully you will see that the beach contains many troughs and steps. On this beach (which is made from pebbles) the steps are large. On a sandy beach the steps will be smaller, and broader.

This ridge was made by spilling waves bulldozing the beach back. It was made near to Neap Tide.

Make a beach

Over the fortnight between the Spring Tides, many kinds of waves will have broken on the beach. Some will act as 'bulldozers' (spilling waves) and some will work like 'rakes' (plunging waves).

Make a sloping beach in a sand tray and then, using a ruler either as a bulldozer or a rake, try to make many different shapes of beach to represent the way the waves shape the beach as the tide moves in and out.

Tidal reach

The various tides allow waves to reach different parts of a beach. For example, at the highest tide the waves can reach right to the top of a beach. Then, as the tide goes out, the waves break on the lower parts of the beach. The lowest and highest parts of a beach are only reworked at Spring High and Spring Low tides.

The lines on this beach show how far the tide has reached during the days before the picture was taken. You can tell the tides were changing from Spring Tide to Neap Tide because each tide has not reached so far up the beach as the one before it. During the week that Neap changes to Spring you may only see one tide line.

Drifting sand

It is easy to imagine how the waves move sand up and down a beach. But on most beaches sand is also moved *across* the beach, that is along the shore.

To see the way that sand moves along a beach – something known as longshore drift – you need some way of tagging the sand.

Tag a pebble

You can follow the movement of beach sand by using a ball that will not float, such as a golf ball.

Tagging works best on a beach that is moderately steep. Place the ball in the swash zone and stand still. Watch how the ball is rolled up the beach, and then back down again. After a few waves have past you should find that the ball has moved some distance from where you are standing.

Ask a grown-up to help you work out how long it would take for the ball to move a kilometre along the beach.

Floating by

Waves and breakers can be powerful enough to carry material along the shore. Try floating in the shallow water of fine weather breakers and you will soon discover that you have drifted along the beach. If you use a snorkel and goggles you can put your face into the water and watch the sand churn over corkscrew-fashion as each wave passes.

You can experience the effect of waves and the sideways currents they make in a swimming pool that has a body-surfing wave machine.

Feel the way you are lifted up and swung gently to and fro as an unbroken wave passes. Then move into the area where the waves are breaking and feel how you are carried forward with the breaker.

Sand tank

You can make a wave generator to watch how waves and beaches form. You need some kind of board that can be moved in and out of the water: this will make the waves.

Cover the bottom of the tank with sand and then watch as the waves move over it. Add some coloured sand to make the movement easier to see.

The slatted wood barriers shown in this picture are called groynes and their purpose is to hold the beach sand in place.

Notice how the sand piles up on one side of the groynes and is washed away from the opposite side.

Many groynes are needed to keep beach sand in place at seaside resorts.

Bars and barriers

Some of the world's biggest beaches make a string of offshore sandy islands. They are called barrier beaches. The barrier beaches that run parallel to the coast from Mexico to Massachusetts, USA are the biggest in the world.

Bars are like barrier beaches that have been forced onto the shore by the waves. The world's largest bar is Ninety Mile Beach in Australia.

Both kinds of beaches contain huge amounts of sand and have often been building for many thousands of years.

This picture shows the kind of bar that forms in places like Ninety Mile Beach, Australia and Chesil Beach, UK.

Barriers

In this picture you can see the hotels and apartments that are built very close to the seaward side of a barrier beach. People can enjoy the long sandy beaches during fine weather, but the buildings may be in danger during a storm when large waves break over the beach.

This picture shows part of the barrier island coast at Cape Hatteras, US. Notice how the barriers have formed well clear of the coast. They were formed just after the Ice Age and have changed little since.

Preserving a barrier beach can be a difficult process because it is always being worked and reworked by the sea.

New words

backwash
the rush of water that flows down a beach after the wave has reached its limit of advance. Much of the surf sinks into the beach, so the backwash is only a small part of the water that rushes seaward

coral
the coral that makes sand in many tropical places comes from broken pieces of coral reef. Coral reefs are made from small animals called corals that make delicately branched skeletons

delta
the build up of sand and silt into a fan shape at the mouth of a river. Deltas give a small idea of just how much material is brought down by the world's largest rivers

dune
a dune is a mound of sand that has been dropped by the wind. There are many shapes and size of dunes, mostly found in deserts. Coastal dunes are often colonised by grasses

energy
the ability to do work. The way that, for example, the energy of the wind can be transferred to waves and therefore drive water onshore. Energy is always transferred, never used up. So when waves break on a beach and the water comes to rest, the energy is transferred to the sand, which then moves

erode
the breakdown and loss of material. Erosion of a cliff takes place in two stages. First the rocks of the cliff are weakened by the constant pounding of waves, then they are carried away by the waves. Beach sand is eroded in one stage because it is already loose material

estuary
the mouth of a river as it enters the sea. Estuaries occur in low-lying areas and they are usually filled with sand and mud

lava
the molten material that flows from a volcano when it is erupting. Lava is orange or red in colour when it is hot and molten, but it soon cools to a black colour

sand
sand is the name for a special size of particle which can be made of many kinds of materials. Mineral sand is mainly made of small pieces of quartz rock that have been broken down. Other types of sand include coral and shell sand, both the broken remains of animal skeletons

sand spit
a long ribbon of sand that stands clear of the coast, but is linked to it at one end. Sand spits usually form when there is a marked change in the direction of the coastline

surface tension
the force that exists when water partly fills a grainy material like sand. The force pulls the grains together, but for it to work the sand must be damp, not completely wet

swash
the rush of foamy water up a beach after the wave has broken

Index

backwash 20, 22, 36
barrier beach 34, 35
bay 10, 19, 34
breaker 19, 20, 25

Cape Hatteras 35
cliff 11, 16
coral 12, 16, 36
crest 23

delta 14, 15, 36
dune 10, 11, 36

energy 9, 36
erode 10, 36
estuary 26, 27, 36

groyne 33
Gulf of Mexico 15

harbour 14
headland 19

lagoon 34
lava 16, 36
longshore drift 32

mangrove trees 27
Mediterranean sea 15
Mississippi river 15
mole 14
mud 12, 14, 26

neap tide 30
Ninety Mile beach 4

pebble 12, 30
plunging wave 22, 30

quartz 13
quicksand 25

ripple 24
river 11, 14, 26

sand 9, 14, 17, 24, 36
sand dune 11, 28
sand spit 11, 36
shell 12
spilling wave 20, 30
spit 11
spring tide 30
storm 22, 28, 30
surf 20
surface tension 24, 36
swash 20, 23, 25, 36

tide 30

wake 21
wave 13, 17
wave generator 32